Zombie Hunterz

Toothless Zombie Hunter Squad

POST APOCALYPTIC FANTASY MODELS

POST APOCALYPTIC FANTASY MODELS

By Harry Pristovnik and Virgil "Dr. Cranky" Suárez

Graphics, Design and Layout: Harry Pristovnik

www.doctorcrankyslabratory.com

Zombie Hunterz

Toothless Zombie Hunter Squad

Styrene Dreams Come True...
Post Apocalyptic Zombie Hunters

Many of us started building models as children, and later returned to the hobby–with the same gleam-in-the-eye fantastical approach to building models...all sorts of models, not only cars. That's how Doctor Cranky started in the hobby at the age of twelve, building model cars and model airplanes, and like a whole generation of modelers, just building and painting them was simply not enough. Thus came the *dreaming* part of building. As a kid, I built entire terrains out in the yard and played with my model cars and tanks and planes, sometimes not only muddying them up good, but also destroying them. I'd bury half of a plane and put grass and twigs and rocks around the area as if the thing had crashed!

It was make-believe inspired by the great box covers of the time–what inspired us to dream *beyond* what came in the box. Later, as an adult, that very same inspiration fueled the kit-bashing, the thinking outside the box mentality that made me dream of other worlds and gave birth to so many zombie hunters, post-apocalyptic, and futuristic models. Kit-bashing (combining parts from several different kits) formed the basis for a great deal of fun–possibly the *most* fun you can have as a model builder.

The question you must answer as a model builder is not how many kits you will build, or what subject matter will repeat itself ad-infinitum, but how are you going to change it up and make your own styrene journey unique? Thus the genesis of the book you are now holding in your hands.

Over time, we became weary of simply painting shiny model car after shiny model car. We respect this style of building–we certainly mean no disrespect when we decided to try something different. Looking at the work of contemporary military model builders led us to a whole new world of weathering, including some pretty cool techniques like using salt to create rusting and chipping on our vehicles. We learned to use an airbrush to create color modulation and texture on our builds. We started dreaming of larger-than-life subject matter.

A few years ago, a friend and wonderful model car builder, Mr. Tommy May, started a thread on one of the forums to see how many builders would be interested in building post-apocalypse zombie hunting vehicles, and the response, simply, was history. Unfortunately, the thousands of responses, pictures, and fun no longer exist because one of the administrators of the magazine (who shall remain nameless) deleted the entire thing, quickly erasing a year's worth of work–eye-popping, jaw-dropping work that fueled the fires of a newly-born subject matter. The following year, I started a thread over at the **Model Cars** magazine online forum, and that thread and all the work is still there for everyone to enjoy and learn from. It's a unique approach to building models unlike any you've built before. Sure, you start with what comes in the box, but you add on, and what you borrow or steal from is only limited by your imagination.

Builders who practice this type of kitbashing and scratchbuilding are a rare breed indeed, because what drives them to create in scale what they imagine and dream is exactly what we all started out to do as builders in our childhoods. We built and played at the fantasy of our vehicle taking flight, or riding over long, winding and muddy roads.

The work in this volume is some of the most exciting and original we've found the world over in terms of this style of building. Our only

criteria, it seems now in retrospect, for including the builds in this book, was simply *originality*. We helped fuel and fan the styrene fevers by looking the world over for builders who were building models so completely different and new that we simply found them irresistible.

Behold the fruit of our labor, or rather the fruit of the labor of all the builders included in this volume. This, so far, is our favorite book because it simply delights us and awes us with so much originality and *different* subject matter. The models showcased on the pages of this volume truly show us a wide cross-section of these builders' imaginations.

The models in this book clearly show how far you can think beyond the kit that comes inside the box. Many of the builders here have borrowed parts from the aftermarket, and even kid's toys! Their love for the "new" is reflected in each and every one of the models showcased here. Many of them clearly had a blast building their models, and each builder has gone out of his/her way to share with us their passion and exactly what it is about their chosen subject matter that drives them to build such unique machines.

Preparing this book has been a labor of love, and we hope that the models we have showcased here for the first time will continue to inspire generations of builders yearning to try their hand and skill at something different. We hope that you will enjoy this book, and that it will light that spark inside your head, and feed your styrene hunger for something new and different.

"Go ahead," Eyegore says, "we challenge you to turn the first few pages of this book and not feel that 'pang' and 'tickle' to build something different of your very own!"

Yes, indeed, that "tickle" you feel is your imagination telling your to move towards your bench, or to at least start dreaming of your own creations and fantasies. This book will feed your hunger, fuel your instincts, and get you jump-started. The rest is up to you.

Add your own creativity to the mix, Crankyhead, and have the most fun you will ever have building a model.

Yours in Styrene,
Doctor Cranky

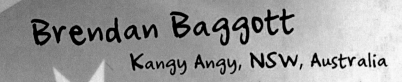

Brendan Baggott
Kangy Angy, NSW, Australia

Brendan's 1949 Revell Mercury zombie hunter has been modified by adding metal armor plate and rivet detail on the outside. The windows have been replaced with scale mesh, and the car features a machine gun and siren from the parts box. The interior is weathered, and includes an oxygen mask and flame throwers. The chassis has been extensively weathered as well. The car was painted with Tamiya primer, then a Tamiya buff color. The car then was heavily weathered with AK Interactive products.

Jaysen Ballantine
Sydney, NSW, Australia

Jaysen's zombie hunter is a Chevy Caprice 4x4 with a truck fuel tank, military surplus gear, water drum, ammo boxes, spare wheels, shovels, tents, bull bars up front, and plenty of lighting to make sure no zombies go unnoticed. The inside is filled with knives, shotguns, hand guns, CB radio, and sleeping bags. With all that gear packed inside, its only a single seater.

JASON BARNETTE
RAVENNA OHIO

"*Valhalla the Zombie Slayer*" consists of a 1954 Chevy Sedan Delivery mounted on a mid 1990s Toyota 4x4 pickup frame, transmission, transfer case, and suspension. Jason's zombie hunter is powered by a Ferrari V-12 from the Pininfarina Mythos concept car. The wheels, tires, and several miscellaneous parts came from a Jeep Rubicon, while the roof cannon, wrecking ball, roof hatch, flame throwers, spikes, skulls and many other detail parts are from the "Warhammer" game. Jason put approximately 110 hours work and well over $125 in parts into this model.

Dan Barten
Wauconda, Illinois

Believe it or not, there's a Revell Ferrari hidden under this *"Road Warrior."* The guns, the trailer base, and the front shield are all from a Tamiya military kit, and the rear tires are from a Iraqi missile launcher kit found in a sale rack at the local hobby store. The smaller tank on the trailer is actually an HO scale railroad tanker car! The Ferrari was altered to imply the metal was getting worn away with use. A hole was melted into the driver's side and extra material added to imply the front fender was damaged in an accident, and then painted black to suggest the damaged fender was replaced. Very creative and unique, Dan!

Curtis Bertschi
Hamilton, Illinois

Curtis took Tamiya's 1966 VW Beetle and built a post-apocalyptic car that he saw as the kind of vehicle that would still be drivable in some none-too-distant dystopian future (or even a backdated dystopian future starting circa 1966 when this car would have been new). He pictured it as a fleet vehicle in service to a large civil-engineering firm, hence the insignia on the doors. Due to the shortage of available gasoline, the car's owner has added a refueling and storage system comprised of a manual pump and barrels. The vehicle shows considerable wear and tear associated with long mileage under inhospitable conditions.

ALESSANDRO BRUSCHI
GENOA ITALY

Alessandro is the Art Director at Auriga Publishing International in Genoa, Italy, so it's no surprise that he has artistic talent! Under all of that scratchbuilt zombie hunting and survival gear, weathering, and rust detail lies the heart of this model, a 1/24 scale Hasegawa Beetle. Very nice work, Alessandro!

Joe Collazo
Sunrise, Florida

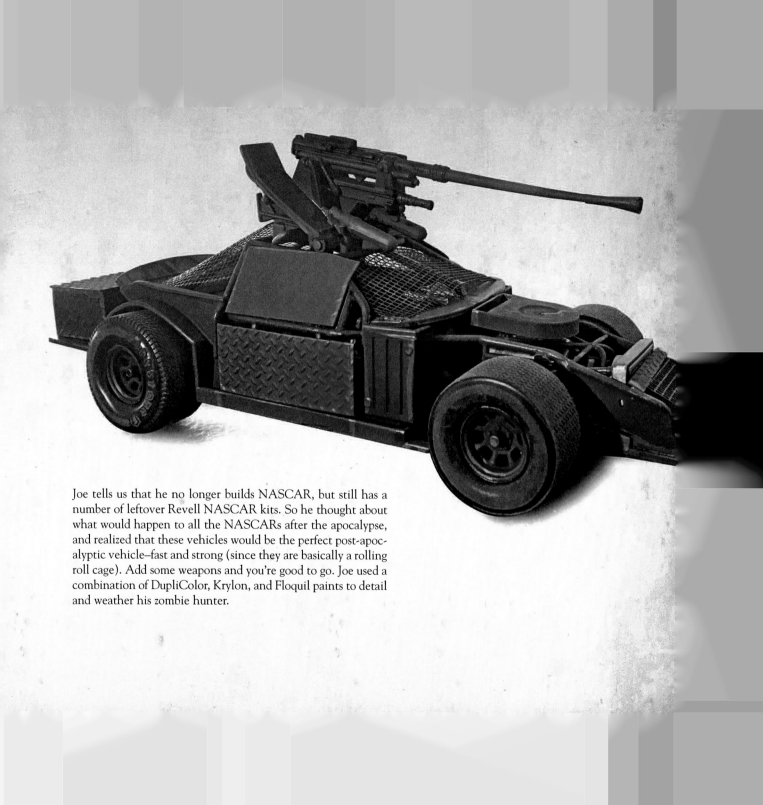

Joe tells us that he no longer builds NASCAR, but still has a number of leftover Revell NASCAR kits. So he thought about what would happen to all the NASCARs after the apocalypse, and realized that these vehicles would be the perfect post-apocalyptic vehicle–fast and strong (since they are basically a rolling roll cage). Add some weapons and you're good to go. Joe used a combination of DupliColor, Krylon, and Floquil paints to detail and weather his zombie hunter.

JOEL COLLAZO
SUNRISE, FLORIDA

BYE BYE, ELMO...

We're not really sure what to say about *"Bye bye, Elmo,"* from the twisted mind of Joel Collazo. Apparently Sesame Street is not the best place to live during the apocalypse. Rumor has it Oscar the Grouch is driving this heavily modified 1/24 scale Fiat 500 that Joel combined with parts from a 1/32 and 1/72 scale tank kit. Elmo (what's left of him, at least) is a cake decorating figure

MIKE DeRAGON

THE BERKSHIRES MASSACHUSSETTS

Talk about clever! Mike's *"Mouse Rod Scout Car"* has a body that was made from a Logitech computer mouse! The wheels, chassis, and engine were taken from an MPC Skorpion. Scratchbuilt or modified items include the Browning M1719 machine gun, bomber seat, engine air scoop, roof, and front "teeth."

MOUSE ROD SCOUT CAR

ANDREY FIRSTOV
CARMIEL ISRAEL

Andrey's 1/35 scale "*Desert Bear Racer*" is mainly used in long-range reconnaissance patrols. The model is a perfect example of kit-bashing and scratchbuilding, as it includes a chassis and roll cage made from left over parts tree sprues! The roll cage, front cover, and trunk are bits and pieces of a plastic toy jeep of an uknown scale.

Wheels came from an ICM 1/35 Ural 4320 truck, while the engine was made from leftover parts of a 1/144 Vostok kit by Airfix. The metal netting on the roll cage was made from an old tea strainer.

Excellent "imagineering," Andrey!

Howard Flowers
Donora, Pennsylvania

The concept here is pretty simple. This is what happens when you get attacked by zombies at a NASCAR track, lock yourself into one of the garages, and modify one of the cars enough so that you can make a run for it. A lot of scratchbuilding went into this model, using styrene, metal, acrylic rod, and resin parts. The paint is all acrylic. And with NASCAR power, you can pretty much bet that you'll be able to outrun all the zombies who may be on your tail!

Matthew Gedert
Columbus, Ohio

Matthew's zombie hunter is based on the Revell 2010 Camaro SS special edition. He raised the suspension and added off road wheels and tires, witha fender flares from the MPC WW2 Jeep. Matthew scratchbuilt front, side, and rear window armor plating. It has the push bumper off the Revell wrecker, with scratchbuilt mini guns where the driving lights would be. The model has a scratchbuilt cargo rack with a scratchbuilt crate, tent and camo roll. The interior is fully equipped for zombie hunting with radios, extra missiles, a sawed-off shotgun, and a machine gun. The paint is a camo pattern with pastel chalks for added weathering effects.

CLINT GORMAN
SUN CITY, CALIFORNIA

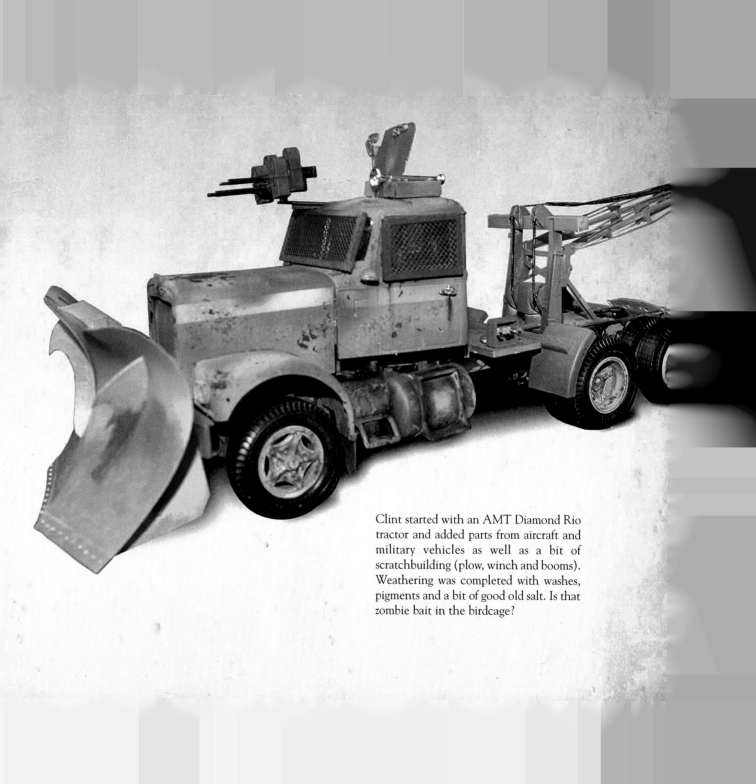

Clint started with an AMT Diamond Rio tractor and added parts from aircraft and military vehicles as well as a bit of scratchbuilding (plow, winch and booms). Weathering was completed with washes, pigments and a bit of good old salt. Is that zombie bait in the birdcage?

Hakan Güney
Istanbul, Turkey

Hakan's *"Doomsday Drifter"* incorporates a "body" comprised of part of the fuselage from Revell's 1/32 SA330 RAF "Puma" helicopter kit, some excellent scratch-built details, and a fantastic weathered look.

Doomsday Drifter

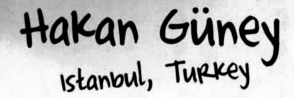

Hakan Güney
Istanbul, Turkey

Another fantastic vehicle from Hakan's fertile imagination is *"Creeping Death,"* which features a body that is actually the fuselage from the Revell of Germany Messerschmitt Bf 109 G-6 kit! The detail and weathering on this model is very impressive!

Creeping Death

Ken Hamilton
Goose Creek, S. Carolina

From the fertile mind of Ken Hamilton comes this flame-throwing defoliation device that began life as a Scale Equipment Limited lawn tractor. After all, we can't have zombies hiding behind bushes, can we? Gasoline stored in the rear drum (supported by the extra set of wheels in the back) is spread for defoliation purposes. The gas is also used for the front-mounted flame throwers.

Ken Hamilton
Goose Creek, S. Carolina

What happens when a fully armored and armed vehicle runs over a nail? Just like everybody else in the real world, you get a flat tire, pull over, jack up the car, pull all the junk out of the trunk so you can reach the spare and change the tire, which is depicted in this diorama. The vehicle is a '57 Chevy with 1/35 scale rear tracks and assorted parts box details. The figure is a modified Tamiya 1/24th scale German soldier.

HEATH HANCOCK

DECATUR, ALABAMA

Heath started with a Revell Dodge Ram, and added parts from the '77 GMC plow truck, including the wheels and tires–and of course, the plow. He added jewelry spikes to the plow to make sure none of the zombies get away! The front of the truck contains a scratchbuilt gas reservoir made from a razor blade container, with added lights from the plow kit as well. The metal screen on the windows was cut from an old screen door. The tarp on the roof covers supplies needed for long outings, with a blanket and chain hanging off the side of the truck and the bed of the truck dedicated for zombie battle. The box in the bed holding the rifles was built from balsa wood. The gun platform was made with old Lego pieces Heath found in his son's closet, a piece of packaging styrene, aluminum tubing, and guns from Tamiya. The model was weathered with acrylics being sponged on in certain locations, and chalks were also used. This was Heath's first attempt at a zombie apocalypse build, and he tells us that he had a blast doing it!

Brian Kirby
Denison, Texas

Brian noticed everyone else was doing the post apocolypse "Mad Max" thing, but no one was going with the survivor thing, so...

"Zombie Apocolypse Survivors Truck"

The Revell '99 Chevy Silverado kit was properly weathering and damage to reflect what the truck would go through as it made its way through the streets and back alleys of the city, as well as the dirt roads of the country. As you can see, the truck has had many run-ins with the undead, as well as some of the living, judging from some of the damage sustained. The "survivor" owner has bedding (felt sheet), a box of canned food (scratchbuilt), and a first aid kit (parts box) in the back seat, and a Magnum and shotgun up front for protection. The machete on the dash is scratchbuilt, as are the rolls of quarters for the shotgun (an idea borrowed from the **Resident Evil** movie). The various zombie parts are from two "mechanic set" figures.

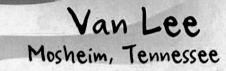

Van Lee
Mosheim, Tennessee

Mike's post-apocalyptic *"Dead Game Hunter"* started with the body of a CHP car, but he scratch-built everything else, including the protective "cage" that surrounds the entire vehicle and protects it from rollovers or zombie attacks. Take a good, long look at these photos and soak in all that detail!

Dead Game
Hunter

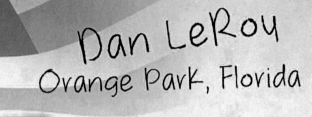

Dan LeRoy
Orange Park, Florida

Dan's heavily armed zombie hunter is a kitbash between a '66 Chevelle station wagon and an M4 Sherman tank! The gun on the hood is from a battleship and Dan's grandson Caleb even contributed with a Lego computer in the front seat. The missiles on the side and the tank on the back are from an F6F Hellcat plane. The tips on the missiles are again from Caleb, from his "Light Bright" toy. It's great to see grandpa and grandson working together to keep the zombies at bay!

Jim Marksberry
Butler, Kentucky

Jim says that these are fun builds to do and bring out your imagination as to what could be. They let you make good use for a kit that is perhaps not up to your standards out of the box, but makes a fine zombie hunter. All the external parts on Jim's model were scratchbuilt. You don't have to buy pre-made parts to build a zombie hunter!

Tommy May
Birmingham, Alabama

The *"Master Blaster"* zombie hunting truck is scratchbuilt, with a selection of various kit bits and pieces sprinkled throughout. The *"Hell-Copter"* and trailer were scratchbuilt using a turbocharged Porsche 911 engine and a Monogram fuel dragster frame and body parts.

This truck/trailer/helicopter combo is a pretty impressive zombie hunting group.

Tommy May

Birmingham, Alabama

Ben McCreghan

Brisbane, Queensland, Australia

The
Zombie Rake

Ben tells us that his AMT '49 Mercury *"Zombie Rake"* was his first attempt at rusting and using the salting technique, and that it was a blast to build, letting his imagination go crazy. And of course, it doesn't hurt to have a mean junkyard dog on your side as you battle the zombies!

Gilbert MonDragon
Chicago, Illinois

Gilbert took the fuselage from Revell's 1/32 scale Bf109g, the wheels from Trumpeter's 1/32 Styrker, and the front and rear axles from Revell's "Real Muscle" 1968 Mustang GT 2 in 1 kit to create this unique vehicle. The rear shocks were scratchbuilt and other bits were lifted from various assorted WarHammer pieces and some resin pieces he had laying about. Some very convincing zombie damage and battle scars finish off Gilbert's wild ride.

Tory Murcaro
Howell, New Jersey

Tory Murcaro's "Zombietle" is a very clever and well thought out example of a zombie hunter. In fact, we like it so much that we thought we'd let Tony himself describe how it came about and how he built his little "über-Beetle." Take it away, Tony...

Tory: "As most of my projects go, the Zombietle came about out of the need to complete a model for a theme build. It is the result of choosing the Revell "New Beetle" snap kit and the color "Silver" in my model car club's annual "Paper Bag Contest," in which club members must determine their project by pulling a random kit and a color out of a paper bag.

I have to admit I had no idea what I was going to do with the kit and color I chose. Then one day I was surfing the net and I stumbled across a rendering of a Hyundai Veloster done up as a zombie apocalypse survival vehicle and the die was cast. It just seemed right–the current zombie craze in both movies and on television seemed to almost mandate it.

So I set about converting my little Revell New Beetle into a force to be reckoned with. I started by framing what would be the armor plated areas with Evergreen .040" square styrene strips. Once an outline was completed, I filled it in with good old Bondo body filler. I cut a circular hole in the rear roof to accom-

Tory Murcaro
Howell, New Jersey

modate the gun turret using my motor-tool. The tube is a piece of styrene turned to the correct diameter on my lathe and glued in place. I framed the windows with Evergreen strips and glued sections of Evergreen styrene tubing in place to anchor the barbed wire. At this point I primed the body to see if any additional filling and sanding was needed. Once the body with its armor plating looked smooth, I added the rivets using a plastic syringe and some Elmer's Wood Glue. Spacing was eyeballed, as I felt if it wasn't perfect it would better reflect how an actual car would be constructed in a post-apocalyptic world.

I bent some soft aluminum .060" rod to shape for the windshield bars using the good old "trial and error" technique. The sandbags were fashioned from Super Sculpy modeling clay, formed to shape over the hood and then removed and baked to harden into their final form. The gun turret, hatch, door flame burners, front brush bar, fender flares and chainsaws were all digitally modeled and output on a 3-D printer. The machine gun and Jerry can were taken from the MPC Hogan's Heroes Jeep kit. The saw blade running boards are cut down plastic knives, and the "teeth" on the brush bar were cut from Evergreen styrene. I left the interior pretty much stock, as it wouldn't be very visible through all the protective window treatments. The barbed wire was hand made using a technique I found on YouTube for making barbed wire for war gaming. The bungee cords holding the sandbags were made from fine soft wire (same as used for the barbed wire) and elastic thread I found at a sewing store.

The body was painted with Tamiya Titanium Silver and Grey Metallic acrylics and cleared with Tamiya Clear Gloss spray. The door graphics were created in Photoshop and printed on Micro Mark clear decal film. They were applied to the gloss coated body, along with the warning markings taken from a spare helicopter decal sheet. When dry, the body was given a coat of Model Master Flat Clear acrylic. Floquil Grimy Black washes were used to bring out the details and black pastel was applied with a fine brush to depict the streaking. When the body looked sufficiently grungy, a final coat of clear flat was applied to seal everything.

The saw blade running boards, door burners and machine gun were painted Tamiya Gunmetal, and the edges of the saws were masked and sprayed with Alclad II Chrome to represent razor sharp metal. The sandbags were painted Polly Scale Mud and given a Model Master Burnt Umber wash.

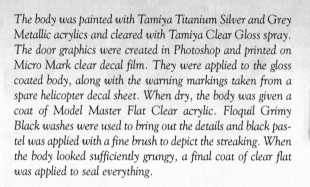

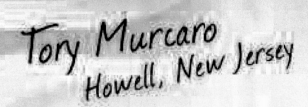

Tory Murcaro
Howell, New Jersey

When dry they were dry-brushed with Testors Light Tan and then given a coat of Model Master Flat Clear acrylic. The Jerry can was painted Krylon Allis Chalmers Orange, given a Grimy Black wash and then a coat of clear flat. The chainsaws were painted Krylon Kubota Orange and Tamiya Bare Metal Silver and weathered with Grimy Black washes over which a flat clear coat was applied.

The wheels and tires are from my spares box and were originally from an Impala SS kit of unknown origin. They were given a coat of Model Master Clear Flat acrylic and the wheels a wash of Grimy Black and then the front wheels were given a light coat of thinned Grimy Black airbrushed on lightly to simulate brake dust. The fender flares were painted Tamiya Grey Metallic and dry-brushed with Testors Steel. Once everything was painted the model was assembled, minor touch up applied and final details applied. I thought about adding some gore, but decided to take the high road so as not to gross anyone out!

Finally the base was digitally modeled and output on the 3-D printer. The road surface is from the kit box bottom with some dried blood spatters added with Floquil Tuscan Red for context (I couldn't resist!). The base was painted Krylon Flat Black and the nameplate letering was airbrushed various shades of green, with a black for the background. The edge of the nameplate was painted Tamiya Grey Metallic.

ZOMBIETLE

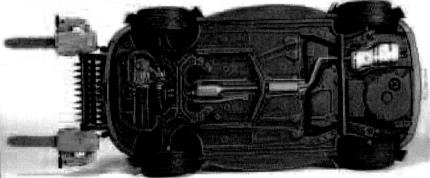

And that's about it. I am delighted it has been so well received. I have to admit it is one of my favorite builds to date. It has a certain charm probably owed much to the little Beetle that lies beneath the zombie killer exterior."

Aleksandr Naydin
Irkutsk, Siberia (Russia)

Take a 1/35 scale Italeri Soviet Katyusha rocket launcher truck, parts of a Tiger tank, and the engine from a children's toy, and you get this amazing zombie stalker. Aleksandr tells us that a vehicle like this would be highly maneuvarable over rough terrain in a post-apocalyptic world, and it would be able to turn and move in any direction at any time... road or no road! This model shows a great combination of clever imagineering, creativity, and excellent, realistic weathering and wear.

Dennis Neal
Shaker Heights, Ohio

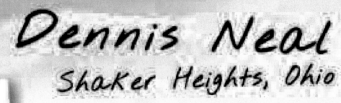

Dennis' 1956 F-100 Pickup is powered by a 427 SOHC engine with dual 4-barrel carburetors. This zombie hunter has four wheel drivewheel drive, a four speed transmission, and is armed with a 106 MM recoilless rifle and a rear mounted .50 caliber machine gun... so that the zombies can be picked off coming and going!

José Ortiz
Pinetop, Arizona

José's *"Zombie Smacker"* began as a Revell 1/24 scale '71 Plymouth HEMI Cuda. The front and rear bumpers are made of pencils and extra sprue from the kit. The drum on the trunk is from a model tank, and the roof rack is made from a chopped up watercolor palette. The inside of the car has duffel bags, ammo bags, an ALICE pack, a first aid kit, and other things Jose made from clay. The tool box on the trunk is a random part from a computer with a pin bent as a handle. José tells us that he ruined the windshield in the process of weathering, but this was a fortunate accident, as the armored plates and hatches were born. Necessity is indeed the mother of invention!

The paint and weathering were done using a mixture of rattle can, airbrush, crushed pastels, and craft paints.

José Ortiz
Pinetop, Arizona

José made *"Cupid"* as a Valentine's Day gift for his wife. The paint job is nail polish. The roof rack is iron wire from the hardware store, the ammo box on top is part of an old computer, and the front bumper is part of a popsicle stick. The model was weathered with a combination of homemade media, Mig paints, and airbrushed Testors flat sand for the dust. The broken-up street is painted plaster, and the water is two part epoxy.

Freddie Peña
Pasadena, Texas

Freddy's '65 Chevelle zombie killer wagon is a barn find that was modified with military grade weapons in the garage of a mad welder. The wagon is designed to run over multiple zombies and has a 360 degree killing zone. The cross hairs allow the driver to aim and shoot without having to adjust anything but the steering wheel!

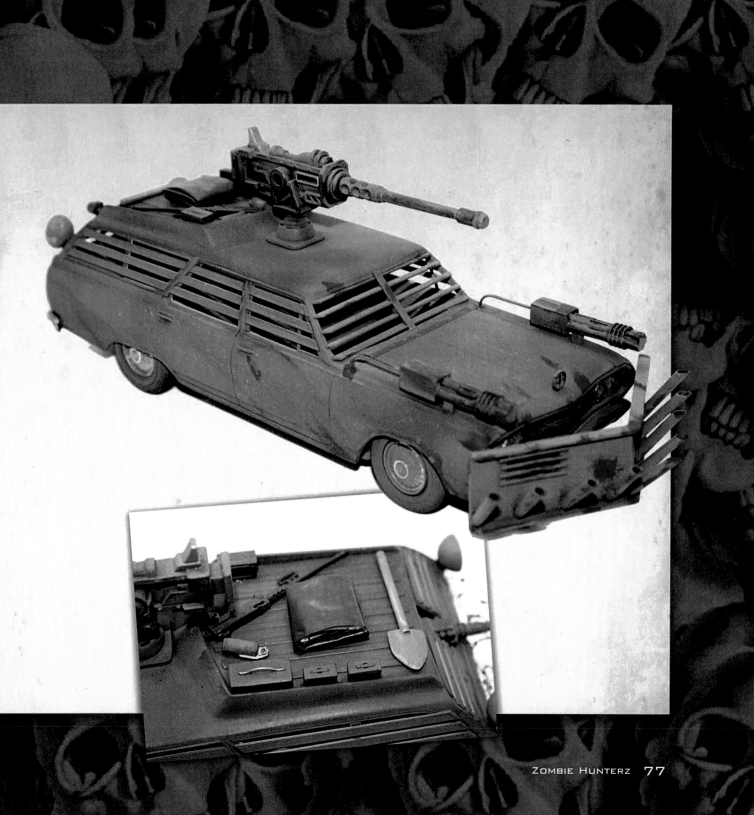

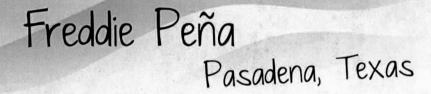

Freddie Peña

Pasadena, Texas

Freddie's *"Zombie Smasher"* is a modified 1997 Ford Explorer 4x4, lifted and fitted with a skid plate. The vehicle has mortar launchers on the fenders, a spiked roller designed to smash and tear apart zombies, and reinforced door panels to pro-tect the front seat occupants. There is a prisoner partition inside the cab to keep captured zombies securely in the back seat. The cab windows and windshield are made from wire form.

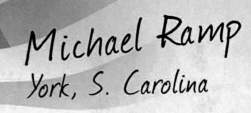

Michael Ramp
York, S. Carolina

Michael's zombie hunter started as a glue bomb AMT '86 El Camino SS. It features scratchbuilt armor, bumpers, and rear turret, and uses a combination of 1/25 and 1/35 scale machine guns. Also on board is a selection of 1/35 scale ammunition boxes, ALICE (**A**ll-purpose **L**ightweight **I**ndividual **C**arrying **E**quipment) packs, duffel bags, sleeping bags, and MRE (**M**eal, **R**eady to **E**at) boxes.

Richard Riscica
North Bellmore, New York

Richard's *"Zombie Killer"* '58 Thunderbird features some serious…uh… "zombie management" tools mounted up front, along with a full complement of more traditional armaments. By the looks of the splatters all over the front of the car, my guess is that the zombie management capabilities of this machine have been very effective!

JOHN ROBBINS
WARREN MICHIGAN

John created his zombie hunter using AMT's 3-in-1 1949 Mercury 2-door Club Coupe. The guns are a combination of parts box items and scratchbuilding, while Warhammer parts were used for the deadly lookinng front and rear ends. The "Feeling Lucky" graphics on the doors came from a sheet of Dr. Cranky's Lab-RAT-ory decals. Nice touch, John!

John tells us the idea behind his zombie hunting Merc idea was that a zombie apocalypse had happenned, and all Johnny had was he grandfather's old Mercury and keys to the local museum!

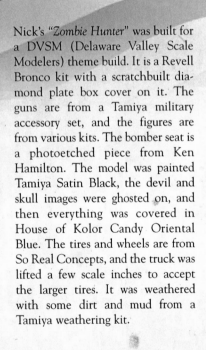

Nick's *"Zombie Hunter"* was built for a DVSM (Delaware Valley Scale Modelers) theme build. It is a Revell Bronco kit with a scratchbuilt diamond plate box cover on it. The guns are from a Tamiya military accessory set, and the figures are from various kits. The bomber seat is a photoetched piece from Ken Hamilton. The model was painted Tamiya Satin Black, the devil and skull images were ghosted on, and then everything was covered in House of Kolor Candy Oriental Blue. The tires and wheels are from So Real Concepts, and the truck was lifted a few scale inches to accept the larger tires. It was weathered with some dirt and mud from a Tamiya weathering kit.

Nick Sandone
Wenonah, New Jersey

Zombie Hunter

Joseph Scroggs
Lexington, North Carolina

Joseph's Tamiya Audi Quattro features aluminum tape on all the windows, missile silos made of drinking straws, and modified gold wine glass wedding favors to make the missles. The skull on the hood came from a dollar store car air freshener that Joseph weathered with shaved black, white and rust colored pastel chalks.

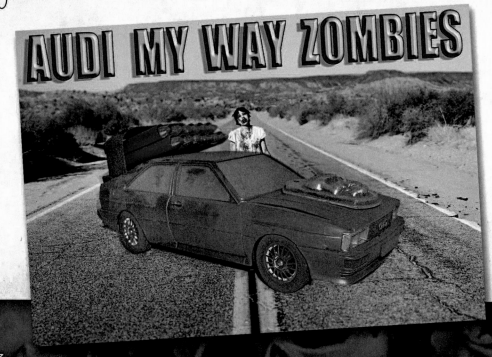

AUDI MY WAY ZOMBIES

Jason Smith
Yukaipa, California

Haunted by his failure to be able to acquire an original Mad Max Police Interceptor kit, combined with the rarity of the kit itself, Jason decided to create his own replica, using Revell's Firebird Street Machine as his starting point.

Jason Smith
Yukaipa, California

Jason's Wasteland '57 Chevy was built using three different Revell kits. It was pieced together from two glubombs and an old unused body that had heat damage. He used the engine from the Revell Henry J gasser.

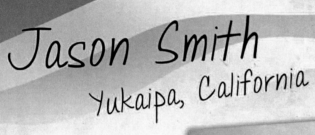

Jason Smith

Yukaipa, California

Jason's Wasteland Toyota Soarer was built from a Tamiya kit. The model features lots of mods, including some photo-toetched parts from a tank kit, and a machine gun that Jason thinks may have come from a small Tonka military toy truck.

Jason Smith
Yukaipa, California

Jason was so excited when Aoishima released the Road Warrior Interceptor kit. He tells us that he's loved this car since he was a kid. This is the one that started Jason's obsession with post-apocalyptic vehicles, and he had to build it!

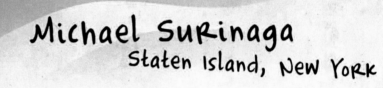

Michael Surinaga
Staten Island, New York

Michael used Citadel paints for the weathering and Active wire mesh for the windows on his Revell 2013 Challenger kit to turn it into a zombie hunter muscle car.

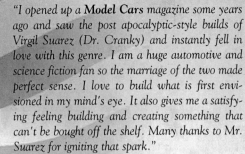

"I opened up a **Model Cars** magazine some years ago and saw the post apocalyptic-style builds of Virgil Suarez (Dr. Cranky) and instantly fell in love with this genre. I am a huge automotive and science fiction fan so the marriage of the two made perfect sense. I love to build what is first envisioned in my mind's eye. It also gives me a satisfying feeling building and creating something that can't be bought off the shelf. Many thanks to Mr. Suarez for igniting that spark."

Carlton Temple
Gibsonville, North Carolina

Carlton's *"Mercenary Merc"* started out as a Revell 1949 Mercury. He scratchbuilt the roof rack and added resin cargo. Home window screen was used for the windows and aluminum tubing was used for the front and rear guns. The extra door plating and rear fuel tank is from Warhammer. The weathering was accomplished using the salt technique and airbrushed acrylics.

Mercenary Merc

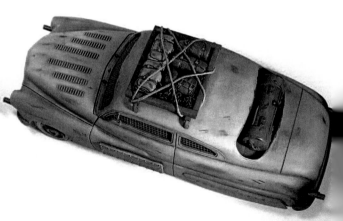

Carlton Temple
Gibsonville, North Carolina

MPC's Roscoe Police Car was the foundation for the *"Zombie Patrol Car."* The salt chipping technique was also used on this build. This car features a photoetched grille, Warhammer bits, and interior details from Carlton's parts bin.

Zombie Patrol

Carlton Temple
Gibsonville, North Carolina

Zombie Shredder

The *"Zombie Shredder"* is the Aoshima RX7, with added fuel tanks and weaponry from Warhammer bits from the parts bin. The front push bar is from the MPC General Lee. The weathering was accomplished by using products from AK Interactive and various airbrushed acrylic paints.

Carlton Temple
Gibsonville, North Carolina

This zombie hunter started as a 1/24 scale Tamiya Mini Cooper. Carlton used the legs and plow from a Heavy Assault Walker by DUST studio. Warhammer 40k bits were used for the door armor and top mounted engine.

The weathering was achieved with the salting technique, various washes from AK Interactive, and airbrushed acrylics. All the stripes and graphics were applied by airbrush.

Mini Stomper

Carlton Temple
Gibsonville, North Carolina

Miss Maybelle

Carlton calls this post apocalyptic build "*Miss Maybelle*." It is the Revell 1950 Ford truck, painted with Vallejo acrylics and featuring an aftermarket resin kit by Dark World Creations. This kit includes the front push bar and resin cargo. Balsa wood was added on the sides for more realism. The large tank in the rear came from the parts bin and the bio-hazard decal came from Doctor Cranky's Lab-RAT-ory.

Carlton Temple
Gibsonville, North Carolina

SCORPION

The *"Scorpion 3DC"* was a collaboration by Carlton and Virgil "Dr. Cranky" Suarez himself. They used the Revell Cuda as the foundation for this project. Virgil scratchbuilt the guns on the front and added extra plating on the top and doors. He also added a digging device on the rear. After spraying a camo scheme paint job, the model was sent to Carlton, who added the driver, interior details, and completed the weathering.

Paul Turley
Tulsa, Oklahoma

Most people build these types of vehicles to do battle with the zombies, but Paul decided to do something different and build a support vehicle. That is why he built the *"Feel Pain"* post-pocalyptic ambulance. The GhostBusters Ecto-1 kit from AMT was weathered using a variety of Ammo by Mig Jiminez products. The wood slats on the roof and front bumper are weathered balsa wood, and the gun on top is from a dollar store toy. Paul tells us that this was a fun build that allowed him to get very creative.

Adam put an Italeri 20' shipping container on an AMT Lowboy trailer pulled by an AMT International Transtar to create his *"Umbrella Corporation"* post-apocalyptic armored container delivery rig. He added armor on all the windows and added an external air filtration system to allow for desert operation. Weathering was done using products from Sophisticated Finishes and MIG, plus chalk dust.

Adam explains that after the apocalypse, trailers full of zombies and/or the infected will need to transported far, far away from the population. This is the vehicle that will do that.

Adam Weinstein
Tamarac, Florida

Megan Welsh

Weeki Wachee, Florida

Megan tells us that she loves *The Walking Dead*– and zombies, period. Her model depicts a farm truck that had been restored by the owner, but over time others captured the truck and altered it for their own uses to keep the zombies under control.

Doctor Cranky's Lab-RAT-ory

We were thinking of Indiana Jones when building this one, and those movies did have an impact on the model type and year for this build. We knew it had to have that '30s retro look but we still wanted to have some sort of zombie hunting feel to it. Were there zombies to hunt back in the '30s? LOL. I am sure there were around and the Nazis collected them all. This is how wacky Hollywood movie ideas are born. Moral of this story: let your imagination roam free and have fun!

RAT KILLERZ

Doctor Cranky's Lab-RAT-ory

Many times, the perfect name and idea comes to mind quite unexpectedly. In this case, I was coming back from my daily walk and near the mailbox I spotted a chicken, and this was my very first thought: Zombie chicken! Then I thought of the idea for this build: what if a chicken was used as bait to attract zombies and then you can easily pluck (pun intended) them off. That easy, and before I knew I was ready for this new Zombie Hunter.

Zombie Baiter

Doctor Cranky's Lab-RAT-ory

We love building Zombie Hunters!

This one was a celebration of the recent re-release of the AMT Gremlin kit. We added goodies from Warhammer 40K, a bit of "gizmology," and threw in our usual amount of watch parts for good measure to create a Gremlin unlike anything that AMC ever built!

MAD GREMLIN

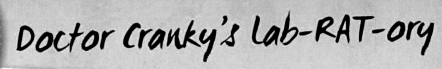

Doctor Cranky's Lab-RAT-ory

The TZH (Toothless Zombie Hunter) is another post-apocalyptic vehicle in Dr. Cranky's ever-growing squad. It is built from the '49 Merc with a truckload of modifications and scratchbuilding. It's the first model to use magnetization on many of the parts for easy swapping. You can play with this model all you want and the look always changes. The engine, made up of a plethora of watch parts and 1/35 scale tank parts and sheet plastic, embodies what Sheperd Payne calls "gizmology." If you are a toothless zombie, you better watch out!

Toothless Zombie Hunter

Doctor Cranky's Lab-RAT-ory

"Sniper" began as the Dirty Donny van, which was heavily modified by cutting a bit more than half off the back and converting it into a zombie sniping vehicle with a scratch-built shooting tower and its own harpoon cannon on the back. We raided our parts box to find just the right elements for this build, including a set of tires from an old Lego set and plenty of Warhammer 40K parts. We wanted the vehicle to look battle worn and road weary, so it was painted and weathered accordingly, using Vallejo and Ammo Acrylics. We left the interior fairly empty because since we covered up the windows and windshield, there was no reason to spend any time detailing the interior, but we did paint the interior black so that nothing would show. The back of the cab is also scratchbuilt so that the crew can travel safely. In a zombie hunting caravan, this vehicle is an asset as it can be used as a fortress and a scouting vehicle. Sniping zombies, of course, is very dangerous, but from a safe distance it can also be quite a bit of fun!

SNIPER

Doctor Cranky's Lab-RAT-ory

Missing from our ever-growing zombie hunting caravan was a fast, modern vehicle that could serve to break up big gatherings of zombies and help clear the way for boots on the ground…so we turned to the new Challenger kit and modified it using spare parts, including some wonderful Warhammer 40K bits. The roller was scratchbuilt and connected via magnets to the front of the vehicle. We also included a heavy cannon on the roof. The tanks over the trunk carry spare fuel for those longer journeys between towns and cities. Zombie hunting has never seen a more devastating machine!

ZOMBIE
CRUSHER

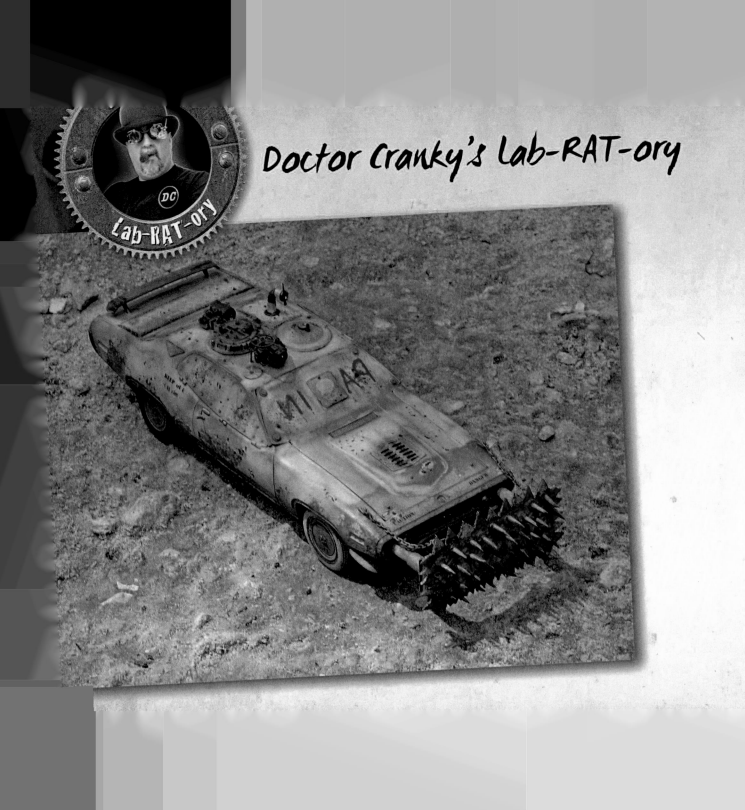

Doctor Cranky's Lab-RAT-ory

Here's a Road Runner like you've never seen before! In a post-apocalyptic world most vehicles would be put together from scavenged parts and pieces. Dr. Cranky created this one with the idea that if he survived World War III, this is the vehicle he would want to drive. One look at your rear-view mirror and you'd be able to see PAIN coming up behind you. What a way to go!

Painkiller

Anatomy of a Zombie Hunter

Part 1: Exorcise Your Imagination...

Over the last decade we've taken a long time to nurture the right elements of our imagination in order to create a rather extensive collection of tips and techniques which we've perfected and utilized in order to build an extensive (and forever on-going) caravan of Zombie Hunting vehicles. Why do we continue to build such vehicles? Because nothing brings us more pleasure and delight! It is as if that part of our imagination has become totally addicted to the process and the adrenaline.

Satisfaction comes to those who are persistent in pushing the bar higher, breaking the boundaries of the routine of building the same vehicle over and over.

With all due respect for those who thrive on building similar looking vehicles over and over, when you build a weathered and story-driven Zombie Hunting vehicle you undoubtedly enter a no-man's land of possibilities rich are the rewards. Fantastic are the discoveries, and the journey—although sometimes quite long—will leave you breathless and content for a long time, extremely proud of having created a model that for a while only existed in your mind's eye, but through dedication and perseverance you brought to life.

This is exactly the story of how **Death Stocker** came about. A while back a friend sent me an old Nascar kit that in turn a friend had sent to him. The kit sat near my bench in the Lab-RAT-ory for a few months until during a conversation with said friend who asked if I had built the kit, he spoke about how these Nascar kits lend themselves perfectly well to turning them into Zombie Hunting vehicles. I opened the box, inspected the sprue trees, and when I saw the roll cage and the chassis, something clicked. Another friend suggested a perfect name for this Zombie Hunter. The project got underway right away.

Building a Zombie Hunter will bring you countless hours of delight. Even your spouse will wonder why you keep walking into the house from the work bench with such a wide smile on your face. Again, although the journey is long and exhilarating because you never know what will come next, it will be some of the most rewarding model building you will ever commit to in your building career. My intention is to walk you through my process so that you can catch the spark of inspiration and build enough determination to build your own Zombie Hunter. Yes, let us start to build this new creation. Get your ideas and your tools and paints and supplies ready… and get ready to build your own. Welcome to the Zombie Hunters Caravan!

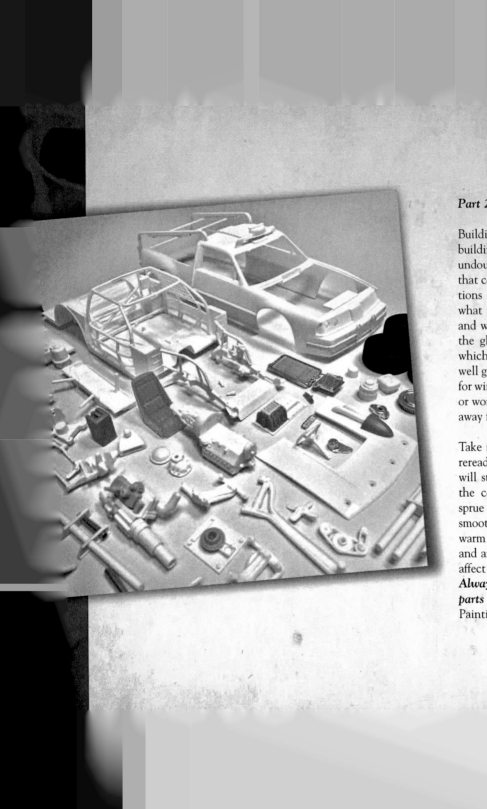

Part 2: Preparation

Building a Zombie Hunter is different from building your standard model in that you are undoubtedly going to push beyond the parts that come in the box. All of the usual preparations apply, of course, including figuring out what parts that came in the box you will use and which you won't (I think immediately of the glass for the front and rear windshields, which I seldom use because I prefer to build well guarded interiors that will have mesh wire for windshields, etc…). The parts you don't use or won't need, of course, you can save and put away for another project.

Take inventory of all the parts, and read (and reread) the kit instructions (the instructions will still be a very handy guide for executing the completed build). Remove any flash or sprue "nubs" from the parts, sand, file and smooth them, and prepare all the parts for a warm soapy bath to remove mold release agent and and any other impurities that might later affect the gluing, priming or painting process. *Always clean your parts. Always prime your parts* (more on that later in the Primer and Painting section).

Prepare the kit the way you've learned to prepare kits for other types of builds. If this is your first time back in the hobby or building models, then you can follow the steps here. Either way we always encourage proper and sound building skills, but with a low stress factor and the highest pleasure and fun quotient for keeping that smile and healthy grin on your face. Indeed, have fun, after all it's just a hobby that you are doing for the pleasure and enjoyment it brings you. We don't build models in the Lab-RAT-ory for competiton. We like to believe we are only in competition with ourself, which is as it should be and it is a way we've managed to learn and enjoy this hobby now for several decades.

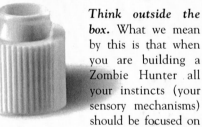

Think outside the box. What we mean by this is that when you are building a Zombie Hunter all your instincts (your sensory mechanisms) should be focused on finding all the right parts–many which won't be found in the kit box you bought, and which will often come from the unlikeliest of places. For example, mesh bags that are used to package onions or potatoes in the supermarket can serve you well as the screen mesh you need for the side windows and rear windshield. Bottle caps or toothpaste tube caps will often make finned brake drums or interesting interior components. Keep your eyes (and mind) open for any item, plastic or otherwise, which you can add to the build to make it look just like that picture you have in your mind's eye. Your imagination is only limited to the distance you are willing to go to find parts.

If you don't believe me, open your refrigerator and look at the caps on your condiments. While you shower, look at the pop-up cap on your shampoo bottle. There's a world of possibilities when you start looking! Look at other kits that you might have, in particular military kits (I know, they are expensive because more often than not they are *Tamiya* or some other Japanese kit brand, but when you need a part, a military kit will come to the rescue) or Gundam kits, or other model car kits: trucks, hot rods, muscle cars…they all have interesting part you can use. About a decade ago we turned to *Games Workshop* and *Warhammer 40K* kits for most of the amazing parts we like to use on our Zombie Hunters. Warhammer 40K kits have become part of our signature style in these types of builds.

In short, keep a nice variety of subject matter in your collection. Even if you don't want to rob the part from an expensive kit, maybe you can make a mold and make a copy for your own personal use. Over the years we've amassed quite an extensive collection of parts from all over the place, and also parts that we repurpose from old electronics: phones, cameras, manual typewriters, and cassette recorders. Watch parts are our favorite, which is why we call them "Cranky's gold." They have been in our arsenal since we started building, and we use them for everything from pulley covers and engine parts to dashboard details, or weapons…there are a gazillion ways of using watch parts.

Prepare and clean all the parts the same way. Clean parts and clean hands keep the process moving forward in the right direction. If you envision a part you don't have or need, then you can always use our method of "gizmology," which is a process that delights us to no end and requires styrene sheet stock, plastic rods, tubing…in short, anything we can use to build whatever we need, whenever we need it.

Keep inventory of your kit parts which you have listed in the kit instructions and also keep a little notebook with your ideas for the parts you are creating. In recent years we've gotten quite a bit of pleasure from building our own weapons, which are easier to build than you'd think.

For inspiration, we suggest you turn to a Google image search to do some basic research, not only for inspiration, but for ideas–in particular when you begin to consider building your own weapons or engine components. Movies like **Mad Max,** **Alien**, and **Death Race** offer great inspiration for ideas. Keep your imagination well fed. Once you have hunted and gathered all your parts, you are ready for the next step.

Part 3: Tools and Materials

Like hunting and gathering parts, preparing your tools and materials will be a lot of fun. When we build Zombie Hunters in the Lab-RAT-ory we do so with the idea that nothing about the build should bring us anything but enjoyment and relaxation. Why stress? More likely than not you already have all the tools and materials you'll need at your disposal: glues, tools like files and clippers and brushes, and all the paint you will need, including primer. If you don't, it probably means that you are just getting started in the hobby and will want to refer to Doctor Cranky's book **Ratz, Rodz and** **Rust: Building Models** **Cranky's Way**, in which we discuss all the various basic, intermediate, and advanced questions and techniques, regardless of when you jump in to participate in this great hobby.

A word about paint. Here in the Lab-RAT-ory, we use a variety of airbrush-ready (properly thinned) acrylics like Vallejo, Ammo, and Citadel Colors (Games Workshop), all of which make the job of painting a model so much easier. Also, because we use an airbrush, the paint helps keep the model looking perfectly in scale and its details sharp and crisp. We also use the airbrush to apply primers, but rattle can primer is perfectly fine, too. If you don't have an airbrush, does it mean you can't build a Zombie Hunter? *Absolutely not.* You most certainly can. Rattle cans are fine and you can still use the salt method (explained in detail in **Ratz, Rodz, and Rust**) to achieve the right rusty and road weary look for your hunter. Again, the idea is to enjoy the process while you build your Zombie Hunting vehicle.

Our basic steps for success are the following: we clean and smooth our parts, bathe them in warm soapy water, rinse and allow them to dry thoroughly, apply primer to all the parts (again, rattle can primer is perfectly fine!), and then we start the painting process. Whether you use an airbrush or spray cans, the system is the same.

In this next part we will discuss some time-saving tips and techniques that will speed up the process and make it more manageable to execute on the way to finishing your first Zombie Hunter.

Part 4: Assemblies and Sub-assemblies

We love to build and work with sub-assemblies. They help simplify the build and make the process more manageable and thus more fun. First we love to mock up the parts and feed the imagination by seeing how things will come together. Again, refer to the instructions unless they are parts you've built from scratch. You can use white glue for the mockup process before you commit to a lasting bond. White glue is friendly because once you are done you can soak the parts in warm water overnight and by morning the parts will one again be glue free and clean. Once we see and know how the assemblies will come together, we like to create a strong bond between the parts by using Extra Thin Glue from Tamiya. We like to see how gradually the parts that will come together get combined into sub-assemblies. The rolling chassis is often such an element. Since we use the airbrush to paint the parts and detail them (you'll learn how in the next part), we don't worry about painting the parts separately. This is very controversial, because most builders learn to paint each part separately and *then* put them together. Sometimes it is extremely difficult to "unlearn" the habits and lessons we've learned and gotten used to... like painting shiny, show quality models. As you will encounter time and again, building a Zombie Hunter is a completely different process–but no less fun and certainly no less rewarding.

Building a Zombie Hunter (remember it should be low-stress, non nerve-wracking, and fun) demands a bit more creativity than normal. Because the builder should always try to think outside the box, we love to assemble our chassis and then paint it. Glueing everything beforehand helps create a strong bond in the parts which will be the foundation of a very rugged and well put together model. All four wheels will touch the ground. The front and rear suspensions will be held in place well. As you will see, the painting process is easier than you'd think and the final results are extremely rewarding–also, mistakes can be hidden very well. So well, in fact, that only *you* will know that you've make a mistake at all! In any case, building assemblies and sub-assemblies gives you an accurate foundation for the rest of the build.

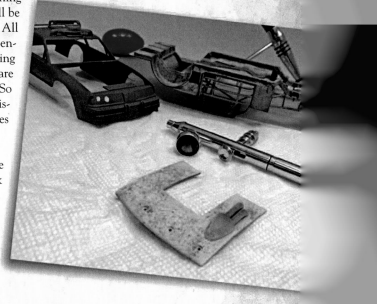

Mocking up is a process by which you assemble the whole model with white glue so that you can see what it will look like (no bad surprises ever). It's like "proofing" your build. You only use plastic cement *once you are satisfied* with each sub-assembly. And once you approve of the way the whole model will look, *then* you will be ready for primer and paint. It's probably not the way you learned to build a model, but trust us here in the Lab-RAT-ory...it works!

Part 5: Primer and Paint

Now remember...the most important thing you ever need to learn about painting your models is that *you must first prime all your parts.* Use a good quality primer. Here in the Lab-RAT-ory we love Plastikote, but other quality automotive brands will also do a great job. Sandable primers go on thin and smooth and they provide a perfect "tooth" for the impending paint to stick to. Without primer, you will always risk chipping the paint, or even pulling it up when you mask. The best policy is to get that extra insurance on your paint job and *use primer*.

Lately here in the Lab-RAT-ory we've been using Vallejo Black/Grey/Rust colored primers and shooting them through the airbrush because we've been paint-ing with acrylic paints

that are pre-thinned and ready for use in the air-brush. The wonderful thing about using air-brushable primer is that you can quickly put down a very thin coat and maintain all your part details really crisp and sharp. These primers are pretty tough too. Your paint coats (and further weathering process) will be safe on an even coat of primer. Regardless of whether you are using a rattle can or shooting your primer through the airbrush, make sure you apply consistent smooth coats that provide full coverage. After all the parts are in primer, I normally like to was them once again in warm soapy water just to remove

finger grease and other impurities. Some builders go straight to the paint.

The more you paint, the better at the process you will become. This is true of using either rattle cans or airbrush. The airbrush is a wonderful tool, but many builders, when they are starting out, hesitate to use it with great anxiety. In the Lab-RAT-ory–after almost 20 years of building and painting models–we still like to use both. When you page through this book you will see a multitude of examples of models that were painted both using rattle cans and airbrush. The models from the Lab-RAT-ory that are featured in this book are mostly airbrushed. The weathering we submit our builds through is more often than not done with the airbrush.

Paint your models to resemble the ideal you have in your mind's eye. Your imagination will not lead you astray. Focus on the final results. Always remember that you can take a brush and some pigment and enhance the colors of the paint you've used. Zombie Hunters are road-weary warriors and more often than not they are banged up and dirty and gunky and they are heavily battle-scarred. Colors will be up to you. What makes these types of build so much fun is your chosen palette. Where are you going to put the rust, the dirt and mud, the zombie blood spatter? This book offers plenty of inspiration, and by now you should know that one of our mottos here in the Lab-RAT-ory is *Inspiration is a two-way street*. And in this case the streets are filled with Zombies, so have fun hunting them down.

You should apply several coats of paint so that when the weathering process begins, you will not risk having something go wrong. If you are going to utilize the salt technique, your first coats of paint after primer are to be rust colored, then you apply water and table salt and then apply your color coat. Repeat the process as many times as you desire to achieve the right look. Again, the salt technique is covered in detail in **Ratz, Rodz, and Rust.** If something *does* go wrong, remember–no stress, no sweat. This is supposed to be a *fun* build. Cover it up with another coat of paint, or better yet, apply a different color to the panel. Most Zombie Hunting vehicles are cobbled together with parts from the builder's parts stash. In short, anything goes. Everything is possible.

Paint all your parts so that everything is ready for assembly when the time comes. For a more extensive look at primer, painting, and paint choices, you should turn to your copy of Doctor Cranky's book **Ratz, Rodz, and Rust: Building**

Models Cranky's Way. Sometimes we like to paint and do sub-assemblies and or build the entire model, and then we begin the weathering and rusting and detailing process. Have fun painting your model. At the end of this stage you will begin to see your imagination and the fruits of your hard work assemble into a model that will have plenty of character. But wait, the fun is just beginning now.

Part VI: Weathering and Rusting

Doctor Cranky is going to let you all in on a little secret that is going to free your mind most of the time while you are at the bench. Ready? There is a multitude of weathering and rusting techniques, and *not one single approach is the right one all the time*. Part of the fun of building models is to keep learning and trying out new techniques. If you put in the time to practice and try out new things, your model tips and technique bag is going to overflow. This is good advice regardless of your current building level.

When using primer and paint, whether you are painting shiny or beaten up, the painting process is way less varied than the weathering process. The weathering process has a larger variety of possibilities and ultimately will add up to countless hours of fun. For example, you can use salt between layers of base coats and this is enough to provide a whole new world of rusting and aging the paint on your models. You can use hairspray to apply a similar effect called chipping. You can sand down from one base coat color to the next. The possibilities are endless. You can play around with pigment powders to get excellent results as well. You can combine everything you learn along the way and arrive at a process that works best for you and the individual style you've developed.

How much weathering is too much? That's for *you* to decide. If you are working off real subjects which you've photographed or seen in magazines for research purpose,s then you will know the look. If you are working strictly from an idea you've had in your mind, then only you know when to hold back. I remember having very lively discussions with other builders about whether chrome rusts or not. Many car modelers will argue that chrome trim doesn't degrade and break down over time, and in time rust. I've taken plenty of pictures of subjects whose chrome (in 40-50 years) has rusted through. The point I am trying to inculcate in you is that there isn't a right or wrong way to the whole business of weathering a model. But I will tell you the number one rule that is that whatever method you use, you must, I repeat, *must* keep the look of the model *in scale*. Too much paint and gunk and weathering and washes can quickly turn your model into one big, goopy mess. Keep developing your eye so that your painting and weathering stay in scale. The airbrush will more than often come to the rescue for you to be able to apply very thin coats of paint.

Here then is a handy list of steps that we keep in mind when we weather our models, in the exact sequence that we employ them:

1. Apply the salt technique as many times as you want, keeping the coats thin. Normally we never exceed three rounds of salting. That's usually more than plenty.

2. If we use the hairspray technique, we always do it after step #1, never before. Chipping fluid or hairspray will keep your paint coats delicate because water, alcohol, and washes (and window cleaner) will reactivate the chemicals and soften the paint. This is the one technique you must use for subtlety in weathering.

3. You can seal the previous two steps by airbrushing a couple of coats of *Future* (now called *Pledge Floor Care*). This is important if you are going to use oil or acrylic washes–and you will.

4. Apply your washes thin and build up the effect instead of adding too much at first. The beauty of washes is that you can repeat the process to build up the effect.

5. You can apply more subtle chipping with a fine brush or with a small piece of a sponge and delicately dab along the edges of panels and seams to get a subtle effect.

6. Finally you can seal in the entire finish on your model with a couple of coats of Dullcote or flat clear. Again, we like to airbrush ours so that the model stays in scale.

These are in a nutshell the steps we take each and every time–and in this order–so that we don't make any mistakes. But if you do make a mistake, rememeber that on weathered subjects, mistakes are extremely easy to fix (or hide).

Now that you have filled your bag of tricks, you can truly have a blast building and weathering your models and getting them looking just the way you like. And if you keep a mirror at the bench and look into it, you will see what a huge smile always appears on your face.

Part 7: Detailing

By the time you arrive at adding the final details, and stylistic flourishes to your model, you've arrived at what we smilingly call *The Zone* here in the Lab-RAT-ory–that place and moment where you catch yourself licking your chops trying not to drool on your own creation. This is the cream, the gravy, the lagniappe of model building. Usually we turn on the music and lean back to admire the fruit of our labor and hard work. But remember this as well–the model is never finished–meaning that your imagination will always trigger more details, more touches you can add later, so you enjoy and delay the moment when you finally call it "finished." Enjoy the process.

If you've made mistakes, this is your chance to fix them–touch ups with a fine brush, getting rid of runaway glue spots with the airbrush. Add a little misted dust to the tires and fog your windshields. The longer you give your model time to sit in front of you, the more you will do to it, and ultimately it's a checklist of things you know the model needs. Take your time, even if it takes days of looking at the model. At this stage of detailing we take time to set up our model in our photography studio and take a few rounds of photos.

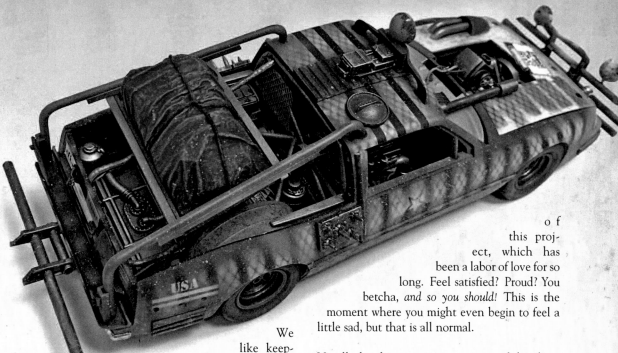

We like keeping the photos on our computer or phone. You'll be pleasantly surprised to find how many things will occur to you to add to the model, including a last minute decal or graphic.

Detailing is a form of signing your name to your model. It's how you mark your style on the work you've done. It's a continuation of the fun you've been having, but now you are preparing to let go of this project, which has been a labor of love for so long. Feel satisfied? Proud? You betcha, *and so you should!* This is the moment where you might even begin to feel a little sad, but that is all normal.

Usually by the most intense stage of detailing, we've already begun to think of the next project, this way one project passes the torch to the next. Building models is a journey, a life-long process that is so gratifying and so enjoyable that you should feel besides yourself when you tell others that you are proud to build models as a hobby. And always remember what the Good Doctor Crankys says: *Inspiration is a two-way street.*

Long live styrene!